Editor
Fiona Macdonald

Text Editor
Jenny Vaughan

Design
Pinpoint/Dave Minchin

Production
Rosemary Bishop

Picture Research
Suzanne Williams

Illustrators
Kevin Maddison
Richard Hook/Temple Art
Ann Baum/Linda Rogers Associates

Consultant
Dr Roger Virgoe
University of East Anglia, Norwich

Teacher Consultant
Christina Morgan

First published in Great Britain in 1984 by
Macdonald & Co (Publishers) Ltd
London & Sydney

A BPCC plc company

Adapted and published
in the United States by
Silver Burdett Company,
Morristown, N.J.

1985 Printing

ISBN 0-382-06833-5

Library of Congress
Catalog Card Number 84-50810

Photographs
Aldus Archive 39B
Bibliothèque de l'Arsenal, Paris. Photo Bulloz 26–7
Bibliothèque de l'Ecole des Beaux-Arts, Paris.
  Photo Giraudon
Biblothèque Nationale, Paris. Photo Giraudon
Bodleian Library, Oxford titlepage (Ms Bodley 264
  fol 266v), 18–19 (Ms Douce 20 fol 132v) 28 (Ms
  Douce 219 fol 55v) 29T (Ms Bodley 264 fol 127v)
  29B (Ms Bodley 264 fol 122v) 41T (see title page)
  43 (Ms Bodley 264 fol 218r) 46–7 (Ms Bodley 264
  fols 180, 65, 76, 181v) 50R (Ms Arab d 138 ff
  199v–120) 50L (Ms Huntington 214 ff 4v–5)
British Library, London. Photo Bridgeman Art
  Library 49 (Add 10302 fol 37v)

Musée Condé, Chantilly. Photo Giraudon-Lauros 8,
  41B
The Masters and Fellows of Corpus Christi College,
  Cambridge 35
Giraudon 39T
A. F. Kersting 38–9
The Warden and Fellows of New College, Oxford 48
Private collection. Photo Bridgeman Art Library 33
SCALA 51
Spectrum Colour Library 42
Victoria and Albert Museum, London 14–15, 19
ZEFA 36
The illustrations on pp. 22–23 have been re-drawn,
with alterations, from those on pp. 8 and 10 of
G. Morgan, Life in a Medieval Village,
© Cambridge University Press 1975, and the
maps on pp. 42 and 52 have been re-drawn, with
alterations, from those on pp. 15 and 25 of The
Penguin Atlas of Medieval History, © Colin
McEvedy 1972.

Everyday Life
The Middle Ages

Fiona Macdonald

Silver Burdett Company

The Middle Ages

This book describes how people lived and worked during the three centuries between 1200 and 1500. These years are often known as the late Middle Ages or sometimes as the late medieval period.

Why *Middle* Ages? Historians use the words to describe the 1000 year period in between the collapse of the Roman Empire in the 5th century and the rapid changes of the 16th century. The early centuries of the Middle Ages were an unsettled time. Invaders from Northern Europe overran many of the lands formerly ruled by Rome. But, by 1200, when this book begins, life for the inhabitants of much of Europe was more settled, even though it was not especially peaceful. There were wars, crusades and peasant revolts. There was plague and starvation and great contrasts in living standards between rich and poor.

However, for most people, life in the countryside, where they worked to grow food, was peaceful for most of the time. Trade flourished and towns grew and prospered. New industries were set up and luxury goods reached Europe from the far corners of the world. Skilled craftsmen built magnificent castles and cathedrals.

We know about life in the Middle Ages from many sources. Thousands of medieval buildings are still standing, and many everyday objects used by both rich and poor people are preserved in museums throughout Europe. Medieval people wrote books and letters about important events as they happened, and many of these have survived for us to read. We can also consult the detailed accounts they kept of their business and farming activities. Even some of the poems and songs which delighted medieval audiences have been preserved in manuscripts, so we can listen to them and enjoy them today.

Contents

The orders of society

Medieval writers divided their society into three main groups which they called orders: peasants (or those who worked on the land), fighting men and the clergy. To explain how they thought these groups ought to work together for everyone's good, they compared society to a human body. Peasants, who supported society by their hard and dirty work, were its feet. Strong fighting men, who defended society, were its arms. Priests, monks and nuns, who spent their lives preaching and praying, were its conscience. The king was at the head of society. Like the body's brain, he was in control of the actions of its head and feet, and was guided by its conscience.

In reality, there were many other groups of people in medieval society. As well as the fighting men, the peasants and people living lives devoted to religion, there were, by 1200, growing numbers of townsmen – shopkeepers, craftsmen, merchants and bankers. There was also an increasingly large group of lawyers and men skilled in administration. In the villages there were woodworkers, potters, thatchers, blacksmiths and ale-house keepers. Women in towns and in the countryside spun wool from which cloth was woven by professional weavers. Along the coast, sailors and fishermen made a living from the sea. There were scholars, artists, musicians and writers. On the fringes of society were criminals – sometimes organised in gangs and living in wild and lonely places – and pathetic outcasts such as lepers. Beggars sought charity wherever they could find it.

So, we can see that when medieval writers described their society, they were concentrating on just the three groups which they felt to be most important. This tells us a lot about medieval society and its values. To them, a hard-working peasantry ensured food and a strong fighting force meant safety from attack plus the chance to make new conquests. The Church stood for high standards of behaviour in this world, and salvation in the next.

▶ Great nobles, or barons, were the descendents of the warriors who had fought so fiercely throughout Europe during the Viking invasions of the 9th–11th centuries. Now they were wealthy and powerful men who lived in fine style on the great estates they had inherited from their ancestors. They had many servants and sometimes even private armies to guard them. Some of them followed their king to war, but, by 1200, most fighting was done by professional soldiers.

▶ Peasants, the largest group in society, worked to produce food for themselves and their feudal overlords. At a time when all work on the land was done by hand- or animal-powered equipment, growing crops and raising animals was an exhausting and very uncertain business – a whole season's crops could be rotted by heavy rain or scorched by a too-fierce sun. For the poorest peasants the threat of starvation was never far away, and there was seldom enough money for anything but the bare essentials of life.

▶ Monks and nuns lived in religious communities – monasteries and nunneries – shut away from everyday life in order to concentrate on their prayers and be closer to God. People in the Middle Ages thought that these prayers were so important that they gave land and money to the Church to help build new monasteries and to pay for their upkeep. Other religious men, priests and friars, lived among ordinary people and hoped to persuade them to lead better lives, by preaching and teaching.

Feudalism

'Every man has a lord to whom he owes loyalty and obedience, and from whom he receives protection.' This was the basis of the *feudal* way of life which existed in most of Europe during the Middle Ages.

Feudal law also applied to the land. According to its rules, every man owed service to his lord for the land he occupied. These services depended on a man's rank, and on the amount of land he held. When a man, rich or poor, died, he could pass his land on to his children, as long as each generation remained loyal to their lord and obeyed the inheritance customs of their locality.

In much of feudal Europe, a land was organised into *manors*. At its simplest, a manor was made up of a big house, where a noble or knight lived, his home farm, called the *demesne*, and the surrounding fields, woods and pasture. A wealthy noble's estate could be made up of several manors – perhaps twenty or thirty. A man who held a manor directly from the king was known as the lord of that manor. In return for their manors, many nobles and knights had originally been expected to serve the king by fighting for him. But by 1200 they usually paid a sum of money to send other men to fight in their place.

The land in the fields belonging to each manor was divided among the peasants. Not all peasants held the same amount of land. Some managed to extend their holding by inheritance or by leasing land from other peasants. In return for their land, the peasants performed labour services for the lord in whose manor their land lay, and sometimes paid a money rent as well. These services included ploughing and harvesting on the lord's demesne, or carrying cartloads of produce. By 1200, these services were regulated by law and by local custom. A peasant who was asked by the lord to perform extra services, or pay an increased rent, could appeal to his fellow tenants and to local documents which recorded past services, for support against his lord.

As well as owing rents and services for their land, many tenants were bound to their lords in another way as well. They were born *unfree*, that is, they could not leave their lord's manor, or marry, or inherit land without the lord's permission. Many tenants resented these feudal demands for their services, and the lord's rights to control their personal lives. Towards the end of the Middle Ages, they began to demand their freedom.

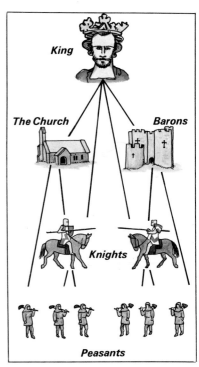

▲ This diagram shows how land was passed down from the king to his lords and then by the lords to lesser lords and peasants. Each layer of the feudal 'pyramid' owed loyalty and service to the one above it. Everyone owed loyalty to the king.

► Each lord of the manor held a court for his tenants several times a year. They were fined if they did not attend. At the court, the lord's steward would hear complaints about any tenant who had not paid his rent or done the correct amount of work for the lord. Questions about the right to inherit land and requests for permission to leave the manor were also discussed at the court.

Courts were often held in the great hall of a lord's castle or manor house, but sometimes in the open air. The artist has based this drawing on an illustration in a 15th century German manuscript.

Village life

For most people in the Middle Ages, 'home' was a village where only about 500 people, or even fewer, lived. The peasants' houses were usually grouped together in two or three streets around the village church, but sometimes, in wooded or hilly country, they were scattered in small hamlets. There might also be an ale-house and a forge.

Each village also had a communal well or stream for water, and perhaps a windmill to grind corn and a big brick oven for baking bread. Often these belonged to the lord, who charged the peasants a toll for their use.

Large, open fields surrounded the peasants' houses and gardens. Land in the fields was often divided into strips. Some wealthy peasants held several strips in each field. Others had only a small amount of land, or none at all. Peasants spent much of the day labouring in the fields, either on their own land strips or on their lord's land. In some villages, the lord's land lay in the open fields by the peasants' land, in others, it was a separate enclosed area.

The peasants helped each other by sharing expensive equipment, such as carts and ploughs, as well as the oxen and horses needed to pull them. At harvest time, it was vital that the whole village worked together to gather the crops quickly, before they were spoiled by rain. If the harvest failed, everyone would go hungry that winter.

The peasants' cows, sheep and horses grazed on the rough common pasture which lay beyond the cultivated fields, and on the stubble of the open fields after the harvest. In the autumn, pigs fed on acorns in the woods.

Peasants without land worked as blacksmiths, wood-workers or potters. Other landless peasants worked as farm labourers for lords or for wealthy peasants.

► **The village blacksmith's forge, where the smith made and repaired all kinds of iron tools and farm implements. Here, the smith is making new shoes for some merchants' pack-horses.**

The agricultural year

January – the lord feasting.

February – too cold to work!

March – pruning vines.

April – gathering medicinal herbs and flowers.

May – the lord and lady hawking.

June – haymaking.

14

In the Middle Ages, farming was vitally important. More than 80 per cent of Europe's population lived on the land. These pictures from a 15th century French calendar show seasonal activities in the countryside. Although the work was hard, the artist has also tried to show that there was some free time for relaxation too – but only for the lords and ladies!

July – harvesting corn.

August – threshing the corn.

September – treading grapes to make wine.

October – sowing corn.

November – gathering acorns to feed pigs.

December – killing the fattened pig.

15

Food and famine

We know from their recipe books that the kings and nobles of the Middle Ages liked rich, elaborate food, that took many servants hours to prepare.

The wealthy could afford to eat plenty of meat, as well as expensive imported luxuries such as sugar, raisins and wine. Instead of plates, they used large slices of rather stale bread. At the end of the meal, these were gathered up and given to the poor, along with other left-overs.

Ordinary people had to make do with very simple food. They ate lots of dark, coarse bread, some cheese and eggs, and vegetables from their own gardens, such as leeks, beans, onions and cabbages. They often made a thick, warming soup called 'pottage' from dried peas. This must

have been very welcome after a hard day out in the fields.

Some families kept a pig, which they killed in the autumn. They hung the meat in the smoke from the fire to preserve it for the winter. Unlike the rich, the poor could not afford large quantities of salt and spices to preserve meat or to disguise the taste when it was beginning to go bad. Rotten meat and mouldy grain often led to sickness. Water, too, could carry disease, as there was no piped water supply.

If the harvest failed or the cattle died of murrain (disease), people might starve unless rich people or the Church helped. Between 1315 and 1320 there were several wet summers, one after the other. Crops failed and there was a terrible famine throughout Europe. One monk, describing the famine near his monastery, reported that some starving prisoners had attacked and eaten their cell-mates. But he may have been exaggerating!

▼ The lord's kitchen was a scene of great activity when preparations for a feast were in progress. Many servants were needed to cook and serve the food. Beggars crowded at the kitchen doorway to ask for scraps from the lord's table. Sometimes, a charitable lady or steward would provide specially cooked soup or porridge for the poor people outside. In nearby storerooms, stocks of provisions would be kept for the winter time, when fresh food was scarce. Large quantities of salted fish, eaten during Lent when meat was forbidden by the Church, were also stored away.

Health and disease

If you had been born into an average medieval family of about five or six children, only two or three of your brothers and sisters would have been likely to survive until you were fifteen. Death was everywhere, whether you were rich or poor. Infectious disease, illness and accidents killed many children. Rich children were more likely to survive because, unlike the poor, they were free from the threat of a lingering death from starvation or malnutrition.

Even if your survived childhood, you would probably have to suffer far more pain and discomfort than we would tolerate today. Women often died painfully in childbirth, and many people spent a miserable old age crippled by arthritis which developed in their joints worn out by a lifetime of hard work.

The Church taught that patience and resignation to God's will during illness was a virtue. This probably helped people to cope with suffering. The Church also taught that it was your duty, if you were fit and strong, to care for the sick and feeble. If you were badly injured or handicapped, or if you were incurably ill with a disease such as leprosy, you would not be able to work. You might have to become a beggar and depend on other people's charity.

Diseases spread quickly and were dangerous because people had little idea of how to prevent them. They did not understand how germs multiplied and were passed on, and they had few effective drugs. Living conditions were often dirty, and germs could breed quickly. Lice and mites lived in people's hair and on their skin. Fleas lived in their thick woollen clothes and among rushes scattered on the floor. These carried disease from one person to another, and from animals to humans. The worst of these was bubonic plague, known to later historians as the Black Death.

In the space of three dreadful years, 1347–49, this disease killed about a third of the population of Europe. It is hard to imagine just how frightened people must have felt when they heard that plague had broken out nearby. Few families escaped without a death, and sometimes the whole population of a village was wiped out. When plague broke out for a second time, it usually killed young children who had no resistance to its germs. People thought that these repeated attacks of plague were a punishment sent by God for their wickedness, and tried to live better lives.

Many peoples' lives were indeed 'nasty, brutish and short'.

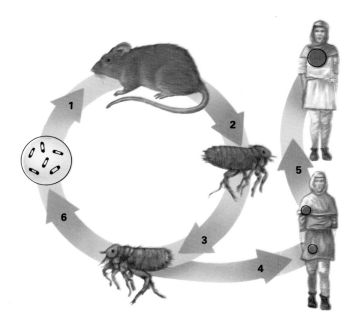

◄ The repeated attacks of plague made people very conscious of death. The skeletons attacking the riders in this French 15th century picture represent sudden death, come to carry off the living.

▲ Plague spread from infected rats to fleas and then to people (stages 1–4). It could also be spread from person to person (stage 5). Infected fleas spread plague wherever they went (stage 6).

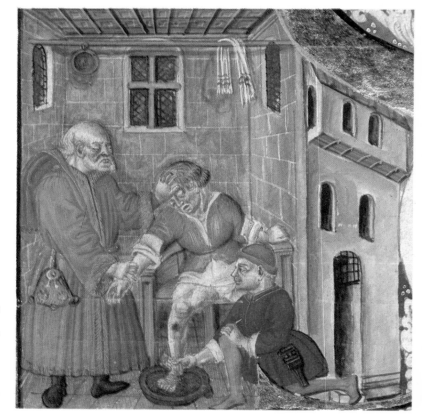

► Medieval surgery was brutal and often fatal. There was no anaesthetic, and patients often died from shock and loss of blood. Infections also killed many people after surgery, since doctors did not understand the importance of keeping wounds clean. Some treatments for illness seem strange to us. For example, the usual treatment for a fever was to bleed a patient, as shown here.

Family life

Few people in the Middle Ages could afford to marry for love alone. The risk of poverty and starvation was always there, so you needed a family to support you if you fell ill. It helped if your family had plenty of money – so people looked for a husband or wife who was comfortably-off as well as affectionate!

Arranged marriages were common among the rich. Children, especially daughters, were expected to obey their parents' wishes. Parents did not think that there was anything wrong in forcing children to do as they were told. They believed that the good of the family was more important than one person's happiness. A family would seek a rich heiress to bring land and money into the family with her when she married their son. Rich women usually married young, and some of them died young, too. This was because they were expected to produce male heirs to carry on the family name, and childbirth could be difficult and dangerous.

Poor people had greater freedom to choose who they married, but their choice was often guided by their need for security. They usually married later than the rich, often not until they were about twenty-five years old, because it took them several years hard work to get all the things they needed to be able to set up home.

Although most couples, both rich and poor, had about five or six children, they would expect only two or three of them to survive. Today, we would be horrified at so many deaths in a family, but in the Middle Ages people accepted it as sad but normal.

Parents hoped that their children would look after them when they were too old or sick to work. Some rich people could afford to retire to monasteries, and pay to be looked after there.

If you were not married, you or your family had to find some way of supporting you. A rich young woman might be sent to a convent if no husband could be found. Poorer people often worked as servants. A widow might make a living as an ale-house keeper, or baker or spinner. Unmarried men could work as labourers, or become soldiers or sailors.

The family educated its own younger members and sometimes children from other families as well. Boys and girls worked around the house, in fields and in workshops, learning skills they would need in adult life.

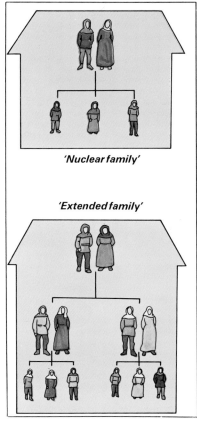

'Nuclear family'

'Extended family'

▲ Top: a 'nuclear' family. In Northern Europe, each couple moved into their own small house when they got married. Their children left the family home as soon as they got married themselves.
Bottom: an 'extended' family. In Southern Europe, people lived in larger groups. All the brothers from one family, with their wives and children, lived together with their parents in one large family house. Only grown up daughters left the family home, to get married.

▲ Children were educated mostly by their parents. Boys from wealthy families would be sent as pages to a noble's castle. There they would learn good manners. They would practise the skills they would need as knights – such as fighting on horseback by riding at a quintain. If they did not hit the shield squarely in the middle, the heavy weight at the other end of the pole swung around and hit them. Girls learned how to read, embroider and play musical instruments.

▼ Children from poorer families also learned skills which would be useful in their adult lives, but these involved harder work. Boys often helped their fathers in the field by leading the plough-teams through the mud. Boys and girls scared away birds from the newly-sown corn. Girls also learned how to do housework, and how to spin and cook.

Houses and homes

If you had travelled through Europe in the Middle Ages, you would have seen houses of many different shapes and sizes. In the southern countries around the Mediterranean Sea, and among mountains, most houses were made of local stone, with tiled or slate roofs. In the cooler north, where great forests provided plenty of timber, houses were usually made from a wooden frame with walls of woven twigs coated with clay and mud and a thatched roof. By the 15th century, people had begun to use baked clay bricks, especially in the towns of Flanders. (Today this is part of Belgium.)

Many people built their own homes, with help from local builders and carpenters. Most ordinary timber-framed houses needed to be completely rebuilt after about 75 years, but brick and stone houses lasted much longer.

Most houses, wherever they were, had only one or two rooms, with perhaps some storerooms and stables added on. In the countryside people spent most of their time out of doors and only came inside to eat, sleep and shelter from the bitter winter weather. In towns, the idea of having different rooms for eating and sleeping was beginning to

▼ Timber-framed houses like this were common in the countryside of Northern Europe. They were built by the people who lived in them, with the help of local craftsmen. Local materials were always used, since the costs of transporting materials from far away were very high. The spaces in between the timbers were filled with woven twigs (wattle) and then covered with clay or mud (daub). The roof was thatched with straw or reeds.

Often, part of the house was used to stable animals, or as a storeroom. Animals helped to keep the house warm, but their dirty bedding harboured disease-carrying fleas.

catch on. In many town houses, the window of the room facing the street had shutters which could be let down to form a shop counter, since craftsmen and traders usually worked at home.

Inside, most houses had a beaten earth floor and a central, smoky fire where the cooking was done. Towards the end of the Middle Ages, more houses had chimneys, which must have made them more comfortable.

The only light in a house came from small windows. These had no glass and the only way to close them was with heavy wooden shutters which kept all the light out. Candles were too expensive for most people, so the amount of time you spent up and about depended on the time of year and how light it was outside. On winter evenings, people sat and talked around the glowing fire, but this did not give enough light to work by.

Furniture was very simple. There might be just one bed for the whole family, with a straw mattress and rough woollen blankets or fur rugs as covers. A family would eat around a trestle table, seated on wooden benches. Chairs were a luxury. There might be one or two wooden chests with locks in which valuable things such as salt could be kept. A few cooking pots, some wooden bowls and mugs and perhaps a bronze cauldron hanging by a chain above the fire, completed most families' stock of household goods.

▼ Once the evening meal was over, the trestle table would be taken down and a thick mattress spread on the earthen floor for the whole family to sleep on. Thick hand-woven blankets or fur rugs would cover the bed. It would be warm to sleep beside the fire, but very smoky.

Castles

War was a constant threat throughout the Middle Ages. Castles were built for defence, but they gradually became more luxurious and comfortable, as lords lavished money on them to display their wealth and good taste. Instead of one great hall, where all the castle's inhabitants could gather for safety behind thick stone walls, separate rooms, still well-defended, were built. There, people could eat, sleep, wash, hold a quiet conversation or receive visitors.

Many people lived and worked in a castle. As well as the lord and his family, and any of their friends or relations who might be visiting, there were dozens of servants and fighting men. Peasants came to the castle to pay their rent. Travelling justices or royal messengers kept the lord in touch with what was going on in far-away towns and cities. Beggars crouched by the gates, hoping for charity.

Organising such a large and complicated household was a difficult job. The noble lady herself was often in charge of all the arrangements, with help from her steward and other servants.

In the castle courtyard there were stables for the lord's horses and kennels for his hounds. Many lords and ladies had a passion for hunting. After the hunt, everyone would gather in the great hall for the main meal of the day, in mid-afternoon. Later, there might be singing and dancing in the glowing firelight.

On other days, the lord would spend time discussing the management of his estates with his steward, or he might visit a neighbouring lord to discuss local politics. The lady might visit the castle storerooms or kitchens to make sure that everything was being done according to her instructions. Or she might read, listen to music, or embroider. But if the lord was away on business or at war, she would take over the running of the whole estate, and would have little time to herself for relaxation.

Castles were furnished with simple and solid wooden beds, tables and benches. Comfortable chairs were a rarity, reserved for the lord and his lady. When the lord and his followers arrived on a visit, the cold stone walls of the castle would be hung with warm and colourful tapestries. These often showed hunting scenes, or romantic subjects. Fresh rushes and sweet-smelling herbs would be scattered on the floor, in place of a carpet. After dark, costly wax candles gave a flickering light.

A wealthy noble would have many houses or castles on his estate, and he and his household would travel from one to another several times a year.

Clothes and heraldry

By our standards, people in the Middle Ages owned very few clothes. This was because clothes were expensive, since they had to be sewn, slowly and painstakingly, entirely by hand. They were often passed on from parent to child, or from a noble lady to her servants as part of their wages. People expected their clothes to last for many years. The poor, who could not afford to buy new clothes, usually had to make do with cast-offs. Only the extremely rich could afford to follow fashion.

Medieval houses were often cold and draughty and so people wore many layers to keep warm. A considerate host offered visitors a thick cloak to wrap around their shoulders while they sat by the fire, to stop the cold air whistling down their neck. In winter, people sometimes wore wooden clogs over their shoes to help them walk in the thick mud.

Clothes were made from wool, linen, hemp and (for the very rich) silk. All these were spun and woven using hand operated spinning wheels and weaving looms. Many ordinary women made their own clothes from fabric they had spun and woven themselves.

Certain countries in Europe specialised in producing particular types of cloth. The best wool came from Spain or England and was sent to Flanders to be woven. There, skilled weavers in the towns belonged to 'guilds'. These were organisations which controlled the quality of the cloth, and made sure that all the weavers produced good work. By the 15th century, England too was producing a lot of cloth. Silks and velvets were made in Italy.

Rich people from Burgundy, dressed in the height of 15th century fashion.

▲ Knights in battle armour needed some sort of badge to show their fellow soldiers who they were and whose side they were on. So each noble family adopted an emblem. This was painted on to their shields and sometimes fixed to their helmets as well. When two noble families inter-married, their descendents liked to shown the emblems of all their ancestors on their shields. By the end of the Middle Ages some of these 'coats of arms', as the emblems were called, had become very complicated. Heralds, who had the job of helping the leaders of armies to organise battles, also took charge of keeping lists of coats of arms.

◄ A market in Bologna (Italy) in the 15th century. Many luxury goods are for sale, including clothes. In the background, you can see a barber's stall.

Poor peoples' clothes were simple and hard-wearing, and far more practical than those of the wealthy.

27

Chivalry and courtly love

Art and music were very popular with nobles and their courtiers. Some lords kept private orchestras to play for them while they feasted or strolled in the pleasure gardens built near their castles. Other lords kept a jester or clown, to entertain their families and their guests. Everyone enjoyed listening to poets and wandering minstrels. Craftsmen worked hard to produce beautiful paintings, tapestries and jewellery for the lords and their ladies.

The favourite subjects for songs, poems and pictures were love and war.

'War is a jolly thing', wrote one fourteenth century French poet. Although, in real life, war was cruel and brutal, the lords and ladies loved to hear songs about the 'chivalrous' deeds of knights in battle. (The word 'chivalry' comes from the French word for knight, and is used to describe the unreal world pictured in poems and songs.) The ideal knight was brave and merciful, and fought only to protect the innocent and helpless. In order to prove that he was worth the name of 'knight', he had to serve many years as a page and then as a squire, learning to fight and proving that he was trustworthy. Unfortunately most knights did not live up to the ideal!

The women portrayed in the romantic 'courtly love' songs of the Middle Ages were as unlike real people as chivalry was unlike real war. In everyday life, both rich and poor women had to work hard, whether in the fields or in their homes, and their husbands and fathers usually controlled their lives. But in the songs, women were beautiful, fragile creatures who existed only to be adored.

Many songs told the story of a young man whose heart was broken by a cruel lady who would not return his love. The lords and ladies listening to one of these songs had probably heard many others like it – but they enjoyed the song all the same, and could admire the singer's skill. It was rather like watching a Western today – we know that the good cowboy will win in the end, but we enjoy the story all the same!

▲ Noble ladies also liked to hunt rabbits and small birds with graceful hawks and falcons. In this picture, a young page is training a falcon to hunt by swinging a 'lure' of feathers high in the air.

Hunting was a favourite activity of noble lords and ladies. Special areas were marked off as hunting grounds, and peasants were forbidden to go there with their dogs. Here, a pack of hounds leaps to attack a terrified stag. A lady follows, blowing a hunting horn.

▲ Four scenes showing courtly amusements, from a 14th century manuscript. A noble lady and a young man talk, tell stories, listen to music performed on various instruments and play chess.

Peasant revolts

Peasants in the Middle Ages had to work hard to grow food, not only for their own families but also for their lord. There were often arguments between the peasants and their lords, but if they were unfree, the peasants had no right to move to another manor, however harshly they were treated.

After the Black Death had killed so many peasants, some lords found it hard to get enough people to work on their estates. The surviving peasants knew that they would be in demand wherever they went, and some moved to different manors. If they were lucky, their new lord did not ask too many questions about whether they were free born or not! Lords increasingly began to employ labourers, paying them wages rather than letting them settle on the land. This was very different from the feudal relationship between lord and peasant, since no vows of loyalty or service were involved.

▼ In 1381, large numbers of peasants marched on London. They had many grievances — some wanted greater freedom from their lords' demands for rents and services, some wanted an end to personal unfreedom, while others wanted higher wages for their work (Parliament had passed laws fixing a maximum wage). All were angered by the government's new tax in 1377.

When they arrived in London, they attacked and destroyed many buildings, including the palace of John of Gaunt, the king's uncle and one of the most powerful men in the kingdom. They also brutally murdered the

Archbishop of Canterbury and many others.

In desperation, the young king Richard II met the rebels twice and spoke to their leaders in an attempt to get them to leave London. At the second meeting, at Smithfield on the outskirts of the City of London, Richard promised to give in to the rebels' demands. But the peasants' leader, Wat Tyler, was killed in front of the rebels on the orders of the Lord Mayor of London. The rebels were furious and horrified, but King Richard persuaded them to return to their own villages, after promising to grant them all their freedom. This promise was never kept.

The countryside became very unsettled. Old families were wiped out by the plague, and unknown newcomers took their places. Gangs of rough labourers, owing loyalty to no lord, moved from place to place looking for well-paid work. People were no longer so ready to accept the old division between 'free' and 'unfree'. Travelling preachers taught that everyone was created equal, and that governments that claimed otherwise should be opposed.

Throughout Europe simmering resentment began to boil over into violence. Sometimes the revolts were led by wealthy peasants who felt threatened by the rapid changes in the countryside. In the towns, demands for higher wages and better conditions led to attacks on local rulers. In France and England, the governments demanded new taxes to pay for wars, and the peasants were roused to fury. In Germany, some peasants tried to set up religious communities where everyone was free and equal.

Everywhere, governments put down the revolts and punished the peasants. But though they seemed to fail, the revolts helped to bring the end of feudalism closer.

War

▲ Joan of Arc was a young French girl who joined in the war against England after hearing 'voices' prophesying a French victory. She was captured by the Burgundians, England's allies against France, and burnt at the stake by the English at Rouen.

▼ The left-hand map shows the lands in France controlled by England at the height of the Hundred Years War. At first the war went well for England, but it was expensive and exhausting to continue. By 1453, England had lost all her lands in France except the town of Calais and its surroundings, as the right-hand map shows.

For knights and fighting men, war was one of the most important things in their lives. There were countless songs and poems about their heroic deeds on the battlefield, and they also looked forward to the chance to take plunder and collect ransom money from the relatives of wealthy captives.

To practise for war, knights took part in 'tournaments'. These were mock battles between two knights. The winner gained great honour and won rich prizes. According to one medieval writer, a true knight 'must have seen his own blood flow, heard his own teeth crack under blows from a fist and, after being thrown twenty times from his horse, have got up twenty times to fight.'

Wars were fought for many reasons. Some were local disputes between two nobles. Some were between rivals for the throne. Others were wars of conquest, or desperate attempts to fight off invaders.

Eastern Europe was constantly threatened by Turkish armies from the Middle East. There were Crusades or 'holy wars' blessed by the Church to drive the Moslem forces from the Holy Land. Towards the end of the Middle Ages, England and France fought for so long that the period became known as the 'Hundred Years War'.

As in most wars, civilians suffered as much, if not more than the soldiers. People living in captured towns were brutally massacred. Advancing armies destroyed crops and set fire to villages. People living in districts where armies were marching were often terrorised by local bandits, who took advantage of the confusion to murder and steal.

Armies were organised under 'captains', who could be

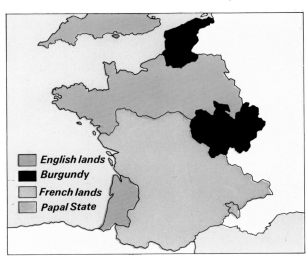

English lands
Burgundy
French lands
Papal State

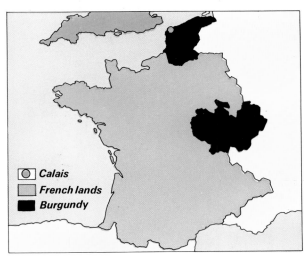

Calais
French lands
Burgundy

either nobles or experienced professional soldiers. Each captain guaranteed to provide a certain number of knights and foot-soldiers for the army, and bargained for their wages with the king. The weapons used were simple but effective. The English longbow was greatly feared. Its arrows could pierce chain mail from well over 100 metres. Knights on horseback charged each other, armed with heavy pointed lances, while foot soldiers fought with vicious pikes. In the 14th century, new weapons such as the powerful crossbow and the cannon were developed.

▲ **Warfare in the 15th century.** This picture from a Swiss chronicle shows two groups of mercenary soldiers in a skirmish. The Swiss were famous as soldiers, and fought in the armies of many European rulers. This picture also shows recently-invented artillery (guns) which gradually replaced bows and arrows.

Government and the law

Under feudal law everyone, from the greatest baron to the poorest peasant, owed allegiance to the king. A criminal was someone who, by doing something wrong, 'disturbed the king's peace'.

Great lords were responsible for punishing minor crimes in their local courts, but serious crimes were dealt with by justices appointed by the king from among his officials and trained lawyers. The sheriff had the job of rounding up criminals and keeping them in gaol until the justices arrived.

Conditions there were usually extremely dirty and crowded and prisoners often died of diseases they caught in gaol before they were brought to trial. While in gaol, prisoners relied on friends and relations to bring them food or money, otherwise they might starve. Charitable people sometimes left money in their wills to help prisoners buy food.

Parliaments started to make laws to deal with particular problems of law and order, such as the way highway robbery increased in the 14th century. In England, the parliament asked lords to cut down all the trees and bushes for 30 feet (about 10 metres) on each side of major roads, so that robbers would have nowhere to lie in wait for passing travellers.

By the end of the Middle Ages, the law had become very complicated, and a new group of professional lawyers grew up. They acted as justices for the king, and also went to court to argue cases for anyone rich enough to pay them.

▼ Gangs of brutal highway robbers were a threat to travellers on lonely roads. Songs and plays told the story of Robin Hood, who stole from the rich to give to the poor. But Robin probably never existed, and most robbers stole for their own profit.

► This picture shows the coronation of a 14th century French king. The king is seated on a throne and is surrounded by bishops and nobles who have sworn to be loyal to him. On either side, two bishops are holding jars of holy oil which has been used in the ceremony to mark him as God's deputy on Earth.

Kings ruled with the help of men skilled in the law and in financial matters. They also called meetings of representatives of the clergy, townsmen and wealthy country gentlemen to discuss important matters such as new laws and taxation.

▼ The punishments for wrongdoing were harsh. People were fined for petty offences, but those who were found guilty of crimes people thought serious were hanged or beheaded. Serious crimes included highway robbery, stealing valuables or livestock, treason and murder. Executions were carried out in public and were often watched by large crowds.

Kings and popes

The ideal medieval king had many virtues. He was a devout Christian, a shrewd lawmaker, a learned man who could encourage scholars and philosophers and a skilful diplomat who could deal with his own quarrelsome subjects as well as dangerous foreign enemies. Some people even believed that because he was God's deputy on earth, a king could perform miracles and cure diseases.

Needless to say, the *ideal* king did not exist. Except in Germany, where a group of princes could choose their Emperor, kingship was usually passed on from father to son. It had nothing to do with ability. Some kings were so weak-minded that their advisors had to appoint a 'regent' to rule instead.

Most kings thought that they should be free to rule their countries as they wished. But the Pope, who was head of the Catholic Church, claimed to have authority over all kings and their subjects.

As God's representative on earth, at a time when almost everyone believed in God and in heaven and hell, the Pope had tremendous power to influence the decisions of kings and their advisors. Enemies of the Church were seen as enemies of God, and the Pope had the power to *excommunicate* anyone who behaved wickedly or defied his authority. (This dreadful punishment meant that they would be excluded from all the services of the Church, and would go straight to hell if they died.) Some Popes even thought that they had the right to remove kings who did not rule according to God's laws.

▶ The Pope was as powerful as any king, and, like a king, lived in great state. This is the papal palace at Avignon, now in France but part of the Pope's own lands in the 14th century. For part of that century, the popes lived in Avignon following quarrels with churchmen and politicians in Rome.

◄ Saint Louis of France was famous for his devotion to the Church. He led his army on a Crusade to the Holy Land, to fight against Moslem forces.

► Henry V of England was famous as a warrior king. He led the English armies to victory against France in the early years of the 15th century.

◄ Duke Philip the Good of Burgundy (an independent state which covered parts of present-day France, Belgium and Luxembourg) was a great patron of learning and the arts. His court was famous as a centre for musicians, painters and scholars.

Parish and people

The parish church was the focal point of the village. Apart from the lord's manor house or castle, it was the largest building. Its wall-paintings, statues and stained glass told the worshippers the Christian story in pictures. This was important, since very few of them could read.

Almost everyone believed in God and in the devil, who lay in wait to tempt people to commit sins. People believed that if they followed the Church's teachings they would eventually go to heaven when they died, and be spared the awful torments of hell. They also prayed to God and to the saints to help them through the troubles of this life. It was a time when scientific understanding of events was, by today's standards, very limited. Therefore, when a child fell sick or a crop mysteriously failed, medieval people looked for an explanation which involved supernatural powers. Sickness could be God's punishment for sin, or perhaps the result of a curse cast by an enemy in league with the devil.

The Church played a part in all the important occasions of peoples' lives. New-born babies were baptised to receive them into the Church. Couples exchanged their marriage vows before God in the church porch. At funerals, prayers were said for the dead person's soul, and their body was laid to rest in the consecrated ground of the churchyard.

The villagers went to church to take part in the services every Sunday, and on other holy days, when the Church forbade them to do everyday work. They could not always understand the services (which were in Latin), but they listened attentively to a good sermon.

The parish priest's duties were to teach the Christian gospel to his parishoners, and to encourage them to live their lives according to God's laws. Many priests were holy men who were loved by their parishioners. Others were lazy and neglected their responsibilities.

In the 14th and 15th centuries, many devout people decided that they would no longer give money to monasteries. They believed that some of the monks had become wordly and lazy. Instead, they gave money to their own parish church, to help with a project such as a new roof. They wanted their church to be beautiful, to reflect God's glory.

At this time, many religious guilds were also set up. Their members promised to help each other if they became ill. They collected money to give to charity and for special services to be said at the altars of favourite saints.

▲ The parish church of Blythburgh, Suffolk. This church was rebuilt with money given by its parishioners during the 14th and 15th centuries. At that time, Suffolk was a very prosperous county. It produced fine wool which was exported to the cloth-making towns of Flanders.

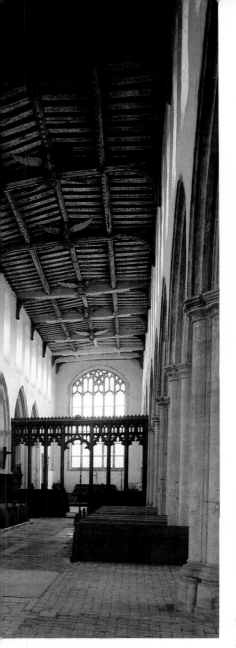

▲ The Middle Ages was a time when many great cathedrals and churches were built. The most skilled craftsmen and stone masons available were employed, since people wanted their church buildings to remind everyone of the magnificence of God and the power of the Church. Many churches are decorated with carvings showing local craftsmen at work. Here you can see masons at work on Florence Cathedral in Italy.

► Four brotherhoods of friars were set up in the 13th century. They were dedicated to preaching and teaching, but, unlike monks they did not live in monasteries. Instead, they travelled from place to place, encouraging the people to lead better lives. This 15th century woodcut shows the Italian friar, Savonarola, preaching to a crowded congregation in Florence.

Pilgrimages

A pilgrimage was a journey to an important religious place. This was usually a shrine where a saint was buried but sometimes it was the Holy Land itself. Every year thousands of people visited popular places of pilgrimage such as St Peter's Church in Rome or the shrines of St Thomas à Becket at Canterbury or St James at Compostela.

The journeys were long and often dangerous. Bandits lay in wait along well-trodden pilgrim routes, and pirates knew that pilgrim ships were easy prey. Even so, many people went on pilgrimages because they believed that the prayers they made at a saint's tomb would be particularly helpful. When people were very ill, they sometimes promised to go on a pilgrimage if they recovered, or they might go to show that they were sorry for their sins. And, with good luck and pleasant company, a pilgrimage could be like a holiday — a welcome change from everyday life. On the journeys, the pilgrims told stories — not all of them religious — to entertain each other, and played games. They travelled mostly on horseback or on foot, staying overnight at crowded inns.

When they reached the town where the shrine was, the pilgrims were met by a whole host of people who made their living from the tourist trade. Some sold holy pictures or little badges as souvenirs. Fake relics — such as bits of pig's bone (supposedly from St Thomas' skull) or splinters of wood (sold as fragments of the True Cross) – sold well. People believed that relics had miraculous powers to ward off devils or heal illness. Other shady characters sold forged pardons or indulgences — documents which claimed to give people forgiveness for their sins or permission to break some of the Church's laws.

Pilgrims, tired and confused after their long journey, were easily fooled by these tricksters. The strange, over-powering atmosphere of the bustling pilgrimage town, with its processions, crowds of visitors and swarms of beggars, would have added to their confusion.

► **Pilgrims kneel before a relic of a saint. Relics were usually kept in special caskets richly decorated with gold and jewels and displayed only on special occasions. People believed that the saints in heaven listened to their prayers and that they would help them here on earth, for example, by curing sickness.**

► **Pilgrims on their way home from a saint's shrine. You can see their wide-brimmed hats which were designed to protect them from sun and rain, and their thick coats. Some pilgrims went barefoot, to show that they were sorry for past sins. The pilgrims in this picture have been to Compostela, in Spain, since they are wearing strings of cockleshell badges, which were sold there.**

Travel and trade

Travel in the Middle Ages was uncomfortable, slow and dangerous. Nevertheless, people often went surprisingly long distances. Merchants traded with far-off cities. Nobles and their households lumbered in convoy from one castle to the next. Soldiers and messengers hastened to join the king's army. Peasants trudged to market, and friars wandered from village to village, preaching their message.

The crumbling roads were full of pot-holes, and often thick with mud. It was usually impossible to go more than 30 kilometres in a day. It took more than a week to get from London to York, and merchants allowed themselves 25 days to reach Bruges from Venice.

Robbers made it dangerous to travel at night, and in some places travellers needed an armed guard even by day. Most people went by foot or on horseback, or used mules or donkeys. Goods were carried in heavy wagons, which lurched and jolted along. It was quicker and safer to send things by river, and most large loads went this way. Really bulky cargoes, or those which had to go a long way, went by sea. New kinds of ships were designed in the Middle Ages, and some could carry up to 1000 tonnes. Sea travel could be dangerous, with storms and pirates, but the important routes between the Baltic and the Asian shores of the Mediterranean were very busy in summer.

▲ This map shows European trade routes in the 15th century. Most goods travelled by sea, but there were also overland routes between ports and the great inland cities.

Many regions began to produce goods for sale to other parts of Europe. By the 15th century, industrial areas such as Flanders could no longer grow all the food they needed, and they had to import grain. Italian ports specialised in trading with Arab lands and with merchants selling silks and spices from the east.

◄ Travel brought increased contact with the Moslem world. In the 12th century, the Arabs had conquered part of Spain, and settled there. They built many beautiful houses in their own graceful style. This courtyard forms part of a palace in Granada.

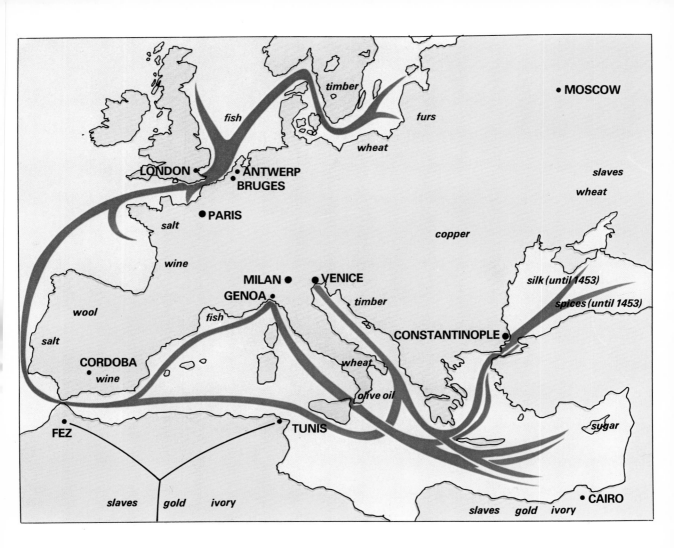

timber

fish

furs

wheat

• MOSCOW

LONDON •
• ANTWERP
BRUGES

slaves

wheat

• PARIS

salt

copper

wine

MILAN •
• VENICE

silk (until 1453)

GENOA •

timber

spices (until 1453)

wool

fish

CONSTANTINOPLE •

salt

wheat

CORDOBA
• wine

olive oil

sugar

FEZ •

TUNIS •

slaves   gold   ivory

• CAIRO

slaves   gold   ivory

► Venice was the 'gateway to
the East'. Her merchants did
business with traders from Asia
and China, and sent ships to
collect goods from ports in the
Eastern Mediterranean. Venice
became very wealthy during the
14th and 15th centuries.

International fairs

A fair was a great gathering of merchants. In the 13th and 14th centuries, the most important fairs were held in the Champagne district of France. Many merchants and bankers travelled through this region along the roads from the north of Europe to the southern ports — where goods arrived from as far away as China. The counts who ruled Champagne wanted to encourage business. So, in return for a 'toll' of goods, they protected the merchants from robbers, provided accommodation in specially built halls, and appointed market bailiffs to make sure that anyone caught cheating was brought to trial. No wonder the merchants found these well-organised fairs a good place to do business!

Each fair lasted about three weeks. The first was taken up with unpacking goods and setting up stalls. During the

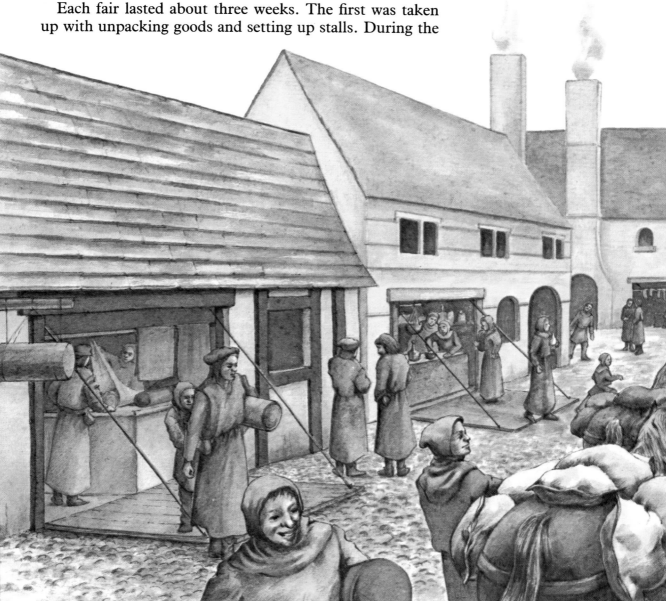

second week everyone had a chance to see what was for sale. The range of goods was enormous. You could buy anything from heavy agricultural machinery made from Scandinavian iron to a luxurious cloak made in Italy from Chinese silk and Russian fur. Merchants also sold raw materials from one country to craftsmen from another. Wool from England and Spain was so highly prized that weavers from all over Europe wanted it.

In the last week of the fair, the merchants finalised bargains and made arrangements for payment. This could be complicated. With money from so many different countries being involved, the merchants had to work out fair rates of exchange. Fortunately there were bankers at the fairs, who could give advice and lend money for more costly purchases. There were also notaries to record details of bargains made between merchants. They made copies of vital documents.

Local tradespeople also did well out of the fairs. Cooks and bakers set up mobile ovens to give the crowds hot food, and the wine shops did a brisk trade.

▼ A packhorse train arrives at a big fair. The traders' stalls are covered with canvas stretched over a wooden frame. The stalls could be taken down quickly and easily to be carried to the next fair.

Fun and games

Life in the Middle Ages was not all hard work! Even the loneliest or poorest peasant could take part in Church festivals, join a marriage or funeral procession, or watch and listen to travelling poets, musicians, acrobats and dancers. Perhaps the village would be visited by a troupe leading a performing bear or dancing monkey. We would think these entertainments cruel now, but in the Middle Ages they enjoyed them very much. Once, some of the king of England's servants kidnapped an ostrich from the royal menagerie and made a lot of money by showing it to astonished villagers, who had never seen anything like it before!

Fun and games were often centred around particular times of year. At Christmas, groups of villagers would dress up as mummers and visit the lord's castle. There they would sing and perform some sketches in return for special Christmas food and perhaps some money. On May Day, young men and girls would get up early in the morning and play games in the bright spring sunlight, before gathering green branches to decorate their homes. It was also a splendid opportunity for courting! Religious guilds (clubs) often put on performances about the life of their patron saint — a popular play told the story of Saint George and the Dragon. They hoped to entertain their fellow villagers, but also to give them a moral to think about on their way home.

There were other festivals related to the seasons and to the agricultural year. Many of these had survived from pre-Christian times and were frowned on by the Church, which was, however, powerless to stop them. At Midsummer, bonfires were lit and various sports and games held. People thought that by lighting a fire when the Sun was at its strongest, they would make sure it returned to ripen their crops the following year.

◄ Musicians, stilt-walkers and a dancing bear from a 14th century manuscript. The people with animal masks are mummers, who performed plays handed down by word of mouth, possibly of pre-Christian origin and thousands of years old.

▲ Plays were usually performed in the open air, on portable stages or even on the back of carts. They were often acted on special occasions, for example, at Easter, when there might also be a fair nearby. Crowds flocked to listen to (or jeer!) the actors, and stallholders did a brisk trade in refreshments.

Education

'Small children are dirty and tedious in infancy and naughty and untruthful when older.' This was the view of one medieval Italian writer. People in the Middle Ages expected their children to be as much like adults as possible. The education they were given was designed to fit them for their place in the grown-up world. By the time they were seven or eight they were expected to be useful members of their family and their community. Nobles' children went to other great houses as pages, while peasants' children worked in the fields.

Most children were educated by their parents. They learned good behaviour and the skills they needed to do the sort of job their parents did, whether they lived in town or in the country. A very lucky boy from a free peasant family might get the chance to train for a career in the Church.

Although some noblemen (unlike their wives) could not read, since they had been educated only for war, others valued learning and sent their sons to Church or monastery schools and the great universities of Europe. Paris was the best-known university, and hundreds of students flocked to listen to the famous teachers there.

The main subjects taught were grammar, arithmetic, geometry, music and astronomy. Students also learned rhetoric and dialectic — the skills of clear and forceful argument. The Church considered all these subjects less important than philosophy and theology, which students were expected to study because of what they revealed about God and the world he had created. New subjects such as geography, zoology, botany and medicine were gradually introduced, but the Church was suspicious of them.

► An alchemist and his assistants, from a 15th century manuscript. Alchemy was an 'unofficial' science. It was frowned on by the Church, and did not form part of any university course. In fact, alchemists were often quite knowledgeable about astronomy, chemistry and herbalism. But their critics said that they also brewed magic potions and were in league with the Devil.
The two assistants are probably apprentices. They were bound to their master for several years, and helped him in his work while he taught them his skills. This was the way in which most craftsmen passed on their knowledge to the next generation.

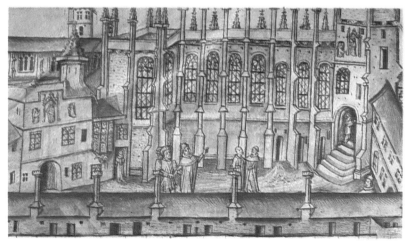

◄ Many colleges at the universities were founded by charitable people, who left money to build cheap lodging houses where poor students could live and study in peace and quiet. This 15th century drawing shows New College, Oxford. You can see the students' individual rooms at the front of the picture.

The new learning

Greek and Roman artists, who lived over 1,000 years before the Middle Ages, had created many beautiful buildings, paintings and sculptures. And Greek and Roman writers had written some very important books about science and philosophy. Many of these books and paintings had been lost or forgotten over the centuries, and the Greek and Roman ways of thought had been replaced by the teachings of the Church. The buildings and statues had decayed until they were often no more than ruins.

In Italy, in the 14th and 15th centuries, artists and philosophers began to take a new interest in the ideas of the Greeks and Romans, and to study with great enthusiasm the ruined buildings and statues around them. They did this for two reasons. Firstly, they were disillusioned with the teachings of the Church. Secondly, they were very excited by what they read in Greek manuscripts shown to them by the Arab scholars who had preserved them in their libraries. Encouraged by the Arab example, Western scholars searched their own university and monastic libraries, and found dusty copies of several forgotten Roman writers. New editions of these were made and copies sent to scholars all over Europe, thanks to the recent invention of printing.

▼ A typical Renaissance painting, by the Italian artist Perugino. It shows a Christian subject – Christ handing the keys of Rome to St Peter – but in ancient Roman style. The characters wear a mixture of 15th century and Roman clothes, and two beautifully-decorated Roman arches stand in the background. Both the people and the landscape shown in the far distance are painted in a very realistic manner.

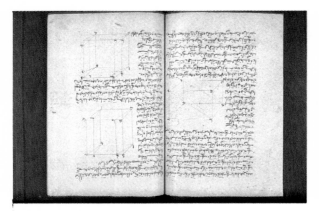

▲ Two Arab scientific books. The Arabs preserved a lot of forgotten Greek scientific knowledge in their libraries, as well as making important discoveries themselves. They were particularly skilful mathematicians, and the left hand picture shows a 13th century maths book. The right hand picture shows 2 pages from a 14th century Arab book about plants.

◄ Humanist artists liked to show great men as the subjects of their paintings or sculptures. This statue shows the famous 15th century Italian soldier and politician Bartolomeo Colleoni. Many artists were supported by gifts of money from wealthy patrons and, in return, produced splendid portraits or statues of them.

The Greeks and Romans had believed that human beings, rather than God, should be at the centre of their thoughts. Because of this, the people who re-discovered their ideas at the end of the Middle Ages are sometimes known as *humanists*. These new humanist beliefs led them to write and paint pictures about human achievements and the beauties of the natural world, rather than concentrating on religious pictures, as was usual in the Middle Ages. This new interest in the world around them also encouraged them to study nature scientifically.

The sense of excitement at these artistic, philosophical and scientific discoveries was so great that people claimed to be living in an age of the re-birth or 'Renaissance' of learning.

Explorations and inventions

Most goods from the East reached Europe after a long journey across the wild countryside of Central Asia. During the Middle Ages, these lands were ruled by Turks and Tartars. Year by year, their armies advanced westward, until in 1453 they captured the important trading city of Constantinople, which guarded the eastern borders of Europe. The presence of warring armies made trade difficult and dangerous.

People therefore looked for new routes to the East which avoided overland travel. Courageous Portuguese explorers made journeys round the hazardous coast of Africa, eventually reaching India in 1498.

Other explorers, excited by stories of these journeys, began to plan further voyages of discovery. Many people told them that the Earth was flat and that they would fall off its edge if they travelled westward! But they persevered with their plans, and the Genoese explorer Columbus set foot on the newly-discovered islands of the West Indies in 1492. We know now that these islands lie between the great land masses of North and South America, but Columbus thought that he had sailed right round the world and had reached islands off the Asian mainland.

The 15th century saw many new inventions, the most important of which was printing. There were also new aids to navigation. And explorers who travelled westward were able to make the long and risky crossing of the Atlantic Ocean because of improvements in ship design.

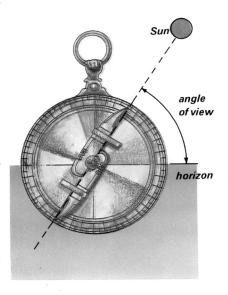

▲ An astrolabe. Invented by the Arabs, it allowed sailors to measure accurately the position of the sun above the horizon, as the arrows on the diagram below show. This was a great help in navigation, since it enabled them to estimate their own position far out at sea.

◄ A German printing press in operation. Printing revolutionised the way in which ideas and information spread. Before it had been invented, books had to be copied out laboriously by hand.

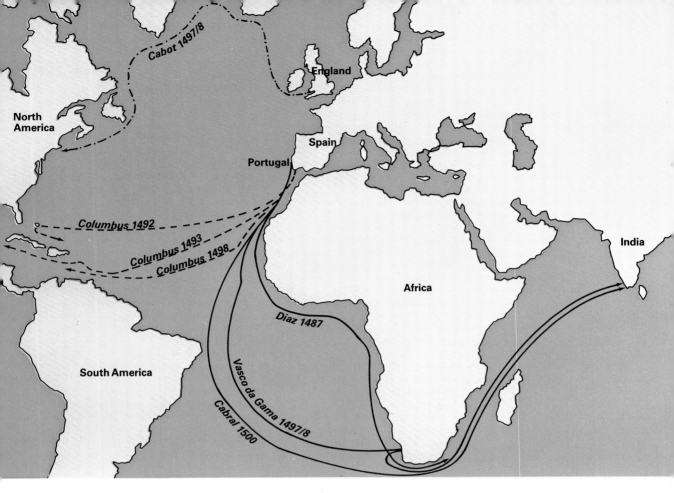

North America

Cabot 1497/8

England

Spain

Portugal

Columbus 1492

Columbus 1493

Columbus 1498

South America

Diaz 1487

Africa

India

Vasco da Gama 1497/8

Cabral 1500

▲ The routes taken by explorers to the East and West before 1500.

◀ A 15th century Portuguese ship. Her fixed rudder and small triangular sail at the back enabled her to sail against the direction of the wind better than earlier ships had been able to do. Ships like this were able to cross the Atlantic.

Town life

Towns grew in size and importance throughout the Middle Ages. Most towns still kept their strong defensive walls in good repair, but, by 1500, people thought of them as centres of trade rather than places of refuge.

A medieval town was not a very comfortable place. People lived crowded together in tall, narrow houses, built above shops and workshops. For ordinary people, these living conditions were dirtier and more unhealthy than those in the countryside. But a wealthy family's town house could be just as luxurious as a lord's castle.

Most houses in towns had no gardens, but only a court-yard with some storerooms and perhaps a primitive lavatory. There might be space within the town walls for orchards and allotments, but there was no room to grow corn or raise animals. Instead, people bought food from countrywomen who travelled in to market each day with baskets of fresh produce.

People went to live in towns for a number of reasons. One was to find work. Within each town, specialised industries such as weaving or leather working developed, providing many jobs. Merchants settled in towns and established businesses. A new middle class of lawyers and bankers set up their offices. People were employed to check the weights and measures in the market, to guard the town walls and gates and even to play music for civic processions and festivals. They all needed food and clothing, so butchers, bakers, tailors and shoemakers set up shops and kept many people busy.

The other reason people moved to towns was to get away from feudalism. The Germans had a proverb: 'Town air makes (you) free.' This was because people in towns owed their loyalty and obedience not to a lord but to the mayor and councillors, who jealously guarded the privileges of their town against outsiders. The mayor and councillors were usually chosen from among the most wealthy merchants and craftsmen. All commercial work was controlled by craft 'guilds' who made sure that their members produced high-quality goods and trained young men in the skills needed for each craft. A man who worked hard and became respected within a guild had a chance of taking part in the government of his town.

Towns also attracted criminals and wandering beggars. Many laws were passed to try and control them.

▲ This picture has been copied from a drawing in a 16th century manuscript. It shows the small town of Feurs in the Forez district of France. The town is typical of a small well-defended town of the Middle Ages. Within the walls, the houses are crowded round the church. The lord's big house stands near the church in the centre of the town. Outside the strong walls with their watch-towers there is a monastery, and also orchards and gardens. The fields surrounding the town are also clearly visible.

The end of the Middle Ages

If an inhabitant of Europe in 1200 had been able to travel forward in time 300 years, he would have found a changed world. Even the countryside would have seemed emptier. Some villages had grown into small towns, but many others had disappeared completely as a result of a gradual fall in population following the Black Death.

Within the villages, too, there had been many changes. Some peasants had prospered and had taken on extra land from new lords. Others had given up their plots of land altogether, and worked for whoever would pay them, for money wages. A few peasants had left the countryside for good and had gone to the towns to live and work. The division of the peasantry into 'free' and 'unfree' mattered less and less.

Fighting men no longer came from among the ranks of the knights and nobles. Instead, paid mercenaries (men who fought for wages) did most of the fighting. They were loyal not to their feudal lords, but simply to whoever paid them. They were rough and brutal men, feared wherever they went. The nobles still played an important part in government, but they had been joined as advisers to the king by wealthy townsmen and country gentlemen.

The Church was being widely criticised in 1500. Scholars and some priests said that monks and nuns were no longer living a life of prayer and service to others. They also wanted to reform the Church's services, and to translate the Bible into each country's own language, so that its teachings could be understood by all without the help of priests.

In some ways, the time traveller from 1200 would have found the 15th century a sad time. People had been depressed by years of plague, and were worried about their sins and frightened of the prospect of going to hell. They welcomed the freedom brought by the gradual decay of the feudal power. But this new freedom also meant that the old world bounded by fixed manorial services and local customs had been shaken.

In other ways, however, the end of the Middle Ages was a time of great excitement and many new inventions and discoveries. Artists in Italy and the Low Countries were producing magnificent paintings and sculptures. The 'new' continent of America was discovered in 1492. Printing had been invented. The Europe of 1500 would have been a fascinating place to visit!

▲ **Mercenary soldiers – fully armed and ready for battle.**

▼ **A 15th century cartoon (redrawn) showing a devil eavesdropping on two friars. The cartoonist was trying to suggest that the friars were so wicked that even a devil could learn from them!**

▲ Three Illustrations from a French manuscript of the late 15th century, showing three different groups in society at the end of the Middle Ages.

Top left: a wealthy noble and his family in their luxurious town house. The room is richly furnished and the family sit at ease on a comfortable settle.

Top right: a craftsman at work in his workshop. His son is helping him by picking up woodshavings from the workshop floor. The finely-carved pieces of wood which the carpenter has finished working on are neatly stacked at the back of the room. His wife is working too – she is spinning with a distaff.

Right: a beggar lies in his tumbledown hovel on the outskirts of the town. His wife kneels in prayer by the bedside. They are both dressed in rags and look thin and haggard in comparison to the elegant noble and sturdy craftsman.

Important events

1202 The *Liber Abaci* by Leonardo of Pisa published. It was the first book to explain Arabic numerals to the west. Previously Roman numerals were used.

1206 Genghis Khan proclaimed 'Great Ruler' by Mongol chieftains. His empire covered much of Central Asia.

1212 Battle of Las Nava de Tolosa in Spain marks the beginning of attempts to drive the Moslem conquerors out of southern Spain.

1215 King John (of England) signs the Magna Carta, an agreement with his nobles to respect the laws and customs of England.

1215 Fourth Lateran Council – an assembly of bishops and cardinals – begins. It examined problems in the running of the medieval Church.

1228 Building work started on the great castle of Angers, France.

1243 Building work started on the Sainte Chapelle, Paris, famous for its stained glass.

1259 Walter of Henly publishes his *Book of Husbandry*. It was a very important and influential work about farm management.

1259 Treaty of Paris signed between France and England. It ensured peace between the two countries for nearly 100 years.

1262 The Italian traveller, Marco Polo, reaches China. He makes a second journey there in 1271.

1277 Edward I of England fights and conquers the Welsh. He starts an ambitious programme of castle building to keep the conquered lands under control.

1275 William de Saliceto publishes the first textbook on surgery and dissection.

1315–20 Famine in Europe.

1327 First reported use of cannon in Europe. They were to revolutionise seige warfare with their power.

1237 King Edward II of England deposed and murdered.

1337 Outbreak of Hundred Years War between England France.

1343 Work started on building the Doge's palace in Venice.

1347 Outbreak of the Black Death. It went away for several years after 1350 but reappeared again many times in the next 150 years.

1356 The *Golden Bull* (a document) issued by the Holy Roman Emperor Charles IV. It gave seven German princes, the 'Electors', the right to choose the next Emperor, and freedom to rule as they wished in their own lands.

1375 The *Catalan Atlas* compiled by Abraham Cresques, map-maker to Peter II of Aragon. It was the first attempt to make a series of maps showing the whole of the (then) known world.

1378 The Great Schism in the Church. There were two candidates for the office of Pope, one supported by the French, and the other by the Italians. Neither side would give way to the other, and so, until 1417, there were two popes. This confusion made the church look ridiculous to many people, and led some clergymen to demand its reform.

1381 The Peasants' Revolt in England. During the 14th century, there were also revolts in France, Flanders and Italy.

1380s The English poet, Chaucer, writes the *Canterbury Tales*.

Famous people

1398 John Hus, an early Church reformer, lectures at Prague University. He was burnt as a heretic in 1415.

1399 King Richard II of England deposed and murdered.

1415 Battle of Agincourt. Henry V of England leads the English to victory over the French.

1431 Joan of Arc burnt at the stake.

1432 The *Ghent Altarpiece* painted by Jan van Eyck.

1446 Building work started on King's College chapel, Cambridge.

1446 Brunellesci's dome at Florence Cathedral finished.

1447 Gutenberg's moveable-type printing press built at Mainz, in Germany. Pictures had been printed by wood-blocks for many years, but it was the flexibility of the moveable type that made Gutenberg's invention so important.

1455 Civil war–the 'Wars of the Roses'– starts in England. Fighting continued on and off until 1485.

1462 Ivan III's empire, based in Moscow, now firmly established and beginning to expand.

1453 The English are driven out of France.

1453 The Turks conquer Constantinople. Soon, they control most of the Eastern Mediteranean.

1478 The Portuguese explorer, Bartolomeo Dias, sails round the Cape of Good Hope at the southern tip of Africa.

1492 Christopher Columbus lands in the West Indies.

1492 The Moslems are driven out of Granada in Southern Spain by King Ferdinand and Queen Isabella.

1498 Vasco da Gama, another Portuguese explorer, reaches India by the sea route.

Philip II (Augustus) (1180–1223) was a French king who created a national army, paid for by taxation, rather than relying on his nobles for their support in time of war.

Genghis Khan (1206–67) created a vast Mongol empire in Central Asia.

Roger Bacon (1214–94) an English monk and scientific pioneer, who believed that observation and experiment were the right ways to gain scientific knowledge.

St Thomas Aquinas (1225–74) was an Italian theologian whose writings shaped the Church's teachings during the later Middle Ages.

Marco Polo (1254–1324) was an Italian traveller who reached China on his adventurous journeys.

Kublai Khan (1260–94) encouraged trade between his Chinese empire and the West.

Dante Alighieri (1265–1321) In his poetry he pioneered the use of the Italian, rather than the Latin, language.

Giotto (1276–1337) was an Italian painter whose attempts to paint in a realistic style make him one of the forerunners of the Renaissance.

John Wycliffe (1320–84) An English theologian who called for reform in the Church and for the Bible to be made available to people in their own language.

Henry 'the Navigator' (1394–1460) A Portuguese prince who encouraged many voyages of discovery and supported explorers with money.

Cosimo de Medici (1389–1464) An Italian banker who was also the virtual ruler of the city-state of Florence in Italy. With his son, Lorenzo, he encouraged many of the best artists of the Renaissance to settle in Florence and work for him.

Botticelli (1444–1510) An Italian Renaissance painter who produced many works of art based on Greek and Roman themes.

Glossary

baron a great lord who held his lands directly from the king.

chivalry the honourable code of behaviour which *knights* were meant to follow.

courtly an elegant style of art and literature far removed from everyday life.

crusade a war against the Moslem peoples who had conquered the Holy Land.

demesne (pronounced 'demean') the home farm of a *lord of the manor*.

feudal a word used to describe the bonds of loyalty and service linking each man to a superior lord.

knight originally someone who held land from the king or a baron in return for performing *military service*. The word later became used as a title of rank or respect.

labour services agricultural work performed by *tenants* on their lord's lands.

lord of the manor a man, usually wealthy or of noble birth, who had been granted a *manor* by the king.

manor an estate comprising lands, buildings and tenants, all under the control of a lord.

medieval a word used to describe anything to do with the Middle Ages.

mercenaries soldiers who fought for pay.

military service fighting for the king when asked to do so, or sending someone in your place. Knights had to perform this service in return for the lands they held.

peasant someone who lived and worked on the land.

pilgrimage a journey to an especially religious place, often undertaken as a kind of holiday.

Renaissance the re-birth of interest in Greek and Roman learning among 15th century Italian scholars and artists.

tenant someone who held land, usually from a superior lord.

tithe a tax of 10 per cent of people's income or crops paid to the Church.

Index

1 2 3 4 5 6 7 8 9 10—WZ—88 87 86 85 84